T0171655

WHAT NOT TO SAY TO SOMEONE NOT EXPECTING

Lisa A. Murray

WESTBOW
PRESS
A DIVISION OF THOMAS NELSON

Scripture taken from the Holy Bible, New International Version®. Copyright © 1973, 1978, 1984 Biblica. Used by permission of Zondervan. All rights reserved.

WestBow Press books may be ordered through booksellers or by contacting:

WestBow Press
A Division of Thomas Nelson
1663 Liberty Drive
Bloomington, IN 47403
www.westbowpress.com
1-(866) 928-1240

Cover photography by Lisa Murray.

ISBN: 978-1-4497-3270-7 (hc)
ISBN: 978-1-4497-3269-1 (sc)
ISBN: 978-1-4497-3268-4 (e)

Library of Congress Control Number: 2011961357

Printed in the United States of America

WestBow Press rev. date: 3/16/2012

CONTENTS

This Book Is Dedicated To . . .

God For giving me His strength, peace, and perseverance at the times I needed them most.

My husband, Sean Who never stopped loving me, taking care of me, and being there for me throughout the whole fertility process and beyond.

My family

My mom, Marilyn Coleman; my sisters, Delyse Coleman-Post and Hily Trevethan; my niece, Lindsay Trevethan; my nephew, Travis Coleman Post; my brother-in-law, Doug Trevethan; my late brother-in-law, Rod Post; my aunt, Dorothy, and uncle, Floyd Kent; and my mother-in-law, Marge Murray-Edwards, and her husband, Frank Edwards, for never being disappointed in me, always loving me, and for taking such good care of me after every procedure and surgery.

My friends

Angie Sartain, Rachel Dwenger, Nola Dwenger, Val Vohland, Peggy Williams, and Lori Moran. They prayed for me, cried with me, held me up when I could not stand, and encouraged me when I felt I had nothing left within me.

Our Pastors and Ministry Partners

Reverend Tom and Tammy Anglin

Reverend Greg and Bonnie Temke

Reverends Danny and Angie Sartain

Reverend Jeff and Rachel Dwenger

Reverend Bobby and Liz King

Reverend Roger and Cheryl Dean

Dr. Patricia Ann Huffmeyer

Raymond Fuchs

For their prayers, hospital visits, support and love. These amazing men and women of God were not only invaluable in *my* times of need, but in Sean's as well.

IN MEMORY OF

Ford L. (Bud) Coleman Jr.: My Dad. Although he passed away December 24, 1985, before my journey was in full swing, his memory helped me through many difficult times.

Rod Post: My Brother-in-Law, My rock, My big Brother, who could always make me smile no matter how much pain I was in.

Waldo Dwenger: Our dear friend who always treated Sean and I like family.

INTRODUCTION

Do you know someone who is having trouble conceiving?
Are you struggling with what to say to your sister, sister-in-law, friend, or co-worker?

You want to help but don't know how. Or maybe you are currently going through infertility treatments yourself, and you're frustrated with the lack of understanding or support from friends and family.

This book is designed to help everyone involved in the infertility process. Read it yourself, then share it with a friend.

THE PURPOSE OF THIS BOOK

Through my sixteen years of fertility treatments, spanning a twenty-two-year period, I learned a great deal about what was helpful and what was hurtful during such a difficult time in my life. Many books, articles, groups, and ministries help people deal with the death of a loved one, fatal diseases, obesity, mental illness, and so on. What is difficult to find, however, is information about how to be helpful and supportive of someone going through infertility.

If you look online for infertility support, you can find information on fertility specialists, herbal fertility treatments, and a lot of medical advice. You will also find some online support meetings, clubs, and infertility quotes. What you won't find is much information on how to be encouraging to someone going through infertility, what not to say, or information leading to a practical understanding of what a woman goes through when struggling with conception.

On November 9, 2004, I made the extremely difficult decision to have a complete hysterectomy. This was in response to my doctor's advice and the choice he gave me of "either have a hysterectomy . . . or bleed to death." Prior to this decision, I had gone through eight surgical procedures, more than six hundred injections, and more than two hundred ultrasounds. My medical bills exceeded $150,000. For twenty years, I had suffered with endometriosis (a medical condition in which the mucous membrane endometrium that normally lines only the womb is present and functioning in the ovaries or elsewhere in the body) and adenomyosis (a benign condition of the uterus in which the endometrium grows into the myometrium (the uterine musculature located just outside the endometrium). There were also surgeries to remove endometriomas, which are a type of cyst formed when endometrial tissue grows in the ovaries, also referred to as endometrioid cysts. These are often filled with dark, reddish-brown blood and range in size from .75 to 8 inches. Although this is a condensed version of what transpired over the twenty-two years, my point is that I learned a lot about people and how difficult it was for them (and for me) to face, understand, and effectively deal with infertility.

I want to be clear about my credentials as you read this book. Although I am a credentialed minister, I am not a doctor or a certified counselor. What you will read comes from firsthand experience and is not meant to treat or diagnose anyone currently experiencing difficulty conceiving. This book is intended to help people better understand and support someone currently struggling through an infertility diagnosis or treatment. I hope this book will also help any woman currently traveling that uncertain path of the infertility journey.

CHAPTER ONE

Understanding Infertility

I n order to know what *not* to say to someone *not* expecting, it is important to first have a general understanding of just how many women are affected By infertility and a basic knowledge of some common terms (a few were stated earlier). It is also helpful to be generally informed of the fertility options available. This information will help you understand exactly what your loved one is facing each day.

According to the National Center for Health Statistics, 7.3 million women, ages 15-44, face impaired *fecundity*— an impaired ability to have children. This accounts for 11.8 percent of the female population. Nearly 2.1 million married women ages 15-44 are *infertile*, defined as being unable to get pregnant for at least twelve consecutive months. Approximately 7.3 million women ages 15-44 have used infertility treatments. To give you an idea of just how common infertility is, it affects one in six couples. So chances are pretty good that you know someone in your life right now who is struggling to conceive.

There are many reasons a couple may be infertile. Although male infertility causes some cases, for the purpose of this book, we will be focusing on female infertility. However, it is important to note that the male of a couple experiencing infertility is also encouraged to undergo testing in order to rule him out as a contributing factor.

For a woman to be diagnosed with an infertility condition, she may undergo procedures such as a physical exam, Pap smear, anal exam, or a transvaginal ultrasound. Two diagnostic tests commonly used for detecting scar tissue and tubal obstruction are hysterosalpingography and laparoscopy.

A **hysterosalpingography (HSG)** involves a series of X-rays taken of the reproductive organs. A dye is injected into the cervix and travels up to the fallopian tubes. The dye enables the X-ray to reveal if the fallopian tubes are open or blocked.

A **laparoscopy** is a type of minimally invasive surgery in which a small incision is made in the abdominal wall through which an instrument called a laparoscope is inserted to permit the viewing of structures within the abdomen and pelvis. The abdominal cavity is distended and made visible by the instillation of absorbable gas, typically carbon dioxide. A diversity of tubes can be pushed through the same incision in the skin. Probes or other instruments can thus be introduced through the same opening. In this way, a number of surgical procedures can be performed without the need for a large surgical incision. Most patients receive general anesthesia during the procedure.

I remember when a doctor suggested that I undergo a series of HSG X-rays. When I heard the term "X-rays," I pictured lying or standing while a machine took pictures, which sounds simple enough. But with this type of X-ray, dye would be injected, so that the doctors could clearly see any potential blockages. I understood the procedure—or so I thought—and scheduled it like most appointments, assuming I would drive to and from the hospital. When I arrived, I was asked to undress and put on a gown, which at this point was something I could do in my sleep. Then I was placed on a metal table where the X-rays would be taken.

My doctor began to explain that first he would be inserting a swab of numbing cream that would help lessen the pain of the procedure. Pain? This was the first mention of pain. After all, I was just having a series of X-rays. As he swabbed my vaginal area with the numbing solution, I tried to keep my mind singing "You Are My Sunshine." This song had gotten me through many postcoital exams (yes, they are just as embarrassing as they sound), catheter reinsertions, IVs, and injections. The nurse, Laurie, held out her hand to me and told me to squeeze when I needed to. I gratefully took her hand with no intention of actually squeezing it. After all, I had made it through many procedures and surgeries, and I was tough. I attributed the warnings of pain to the insertion the syringe of dye into my inverted uterus; once the dye was completely inserted, I assumed I would be on the home stretch, with only the clicking of the X-rays remaining.

Once the syringe was completely inserted, my doctor made another statement I was not prepared for. He told me that many of his patients underwent general anesthesia for this procedure due to the pain level, but he knew that I was tough and would be able to handle it when he injected the dye. What? The pain wasn't over? It hadn't even started yet?

For the first time ever, I wanted to just stop—to pull out the syringe, grab my clothes, and run. I had been tough— many times. I also usually had my husband present to support me. But this was just an X-ray; I had told him not to take off work, that I would be fine going alone. After all, did I mention it was just X-rays?

My doctor continued to tell me that he was going to start injecting the dye and that I would begin to feel mild cramping. Laurie began to squeeze my hand. That was never a good sign . . . what did she know that I didn't?

"Here we go," he said as he began to inject what felt like pure acid running quickly up into my uterus. It put me in so much pain so quickly that I couldn't breathe. I could hear Laurie and my doctor telling me to "just breathe," but I couldn't. Tears streamed down the sides of my face, and then all I heard was screaming . . . and it was me. I tried to stop but couldn't. I kept squeezing Laurie's hand harder and harder. Meanwhile, she was trying to hold me still so the X-rays could be taken, but everything within me wanted to crawl into the fetal position and scream for Sean, my husband.

What seemed like an eternity later, the syringe was removed, and my doctor told me to just rest until I was ready to get dressed. Part of me wanted to lie there forever, and part of me wanted to run home and crawl into bed and cry.

Laurie helped me up as I apologized for squeezing her hand so hard. She wanted me to sit longer and make sure I was ready to walk, but I just wanted to leave. I stood up, and my legs shook. Tears flooded my eyes as I attempted to walk normally out of the room, down the hall, and out to the parking lot to my car. My walk was more like a shuffle; pain followed each movement.

After stopping at several benches to rest, I finally made it to my car. It was all I could do to actually get into the car and sit down, but once there, in the safety and privacy of my car . . . I broke down. I cried for a long time. I'm not sure what I was the most upset about: how unprepared I had been for the procedure, how alone I had been for the procedure, or how very tired I was of procedures. Not to mention the intense pain that was causing sweat to run down my face and back. I was still shaking; my legs were weak, like overcooked spaghetti; and the dye was still oozing out of me as I sat there wishing I could just beam myself home.

Minutes later I pulled into our driveway and slowly made it up the stairs. Sean called me shortly after crawling into bed to see how the X-rays went, and all I could do was cry. He came right home.

So why am I recollecting this particularly harrowing procedure for you? Because I think it is important to understand that you never know what your loved one has just gone through. Even a series of seemingly simple X-rays can actually be a traumatic event in her life. I remember this day as if it were yesterday, and it was seven years ago. It wasn't the doctor's fault (although in retrospect, if the general anesthesia had been offered, I would have jumped at it); both he and his nurse were kind and compassionate. Every woman is different. Every woman's body is different. Every woman's emotions are different. Everyone reacts differently to tests, stress, pain, and procedures. What was excruciating for me may have not been as painful for another woman. What a woman experiences throughout the fertility journey cannot be measured from one person to the next. I cannot stress this enough. Someone else's ability to breeze through an HSG does not downplay what I went through. When approaching the topic of infertility with someone you know is enduring it, remember that her journey is her own, and the pain is her own. No one can possibly walk in her exact footsteps.

CHAPTER TWO

Once Diagnosed with Infertility

N

o woman expects to be diagnosed with infertility. All of us just expect that when we are ready to have children, we will simply go off any birth control we may be on, and in a reasonable amount of time, we will have a joyous occasion to celebrate.

Lori is a friend of mine whom I have known my whole life. I vividly remember a conversation we had once. It seems like only yesterday that she told me, "It is time." I asked her what she meant, and she said that it was time have children. She then described to me just how she would achieve becoming pregnant.

"I have it all planned out," she shared. "I am ovulating today, so I'm making Chuck's favorite dinner. I'm going to light candles, and I have some music ready. Tonight is the night I am going to get pregnant with our first child."

Wow . . . I was amazed. "So this is what people do when they are ready to have a child!" I thought. The really amazing part of this story is that it happened just as she said it would: Lori got pregnant that night! Nine months later, she gave birth to her son David. When they decided it was time for a sibling, Lori repeated the process, and they had their second son, Derek.

For many women, it really is that easy. So, of course, I thought that when the time came, it would be that easy for me, too. When you begin to struggle with becoming pregnant, you start to wonder why. After all, 14 percent of pregnancies are unwanted by the mother. Many women are having abortions. Babies are being abused and even murdered. Why, then, are women in loving homes and loving families unable to conceive? These are just some of the thoughts that can run through a woman's mind while in the beginning stage of the fertility diagnosis.

Both the man and woman go through a series of blood tests, sperm-count tests, and several or all of the diagnostic procedures described previously. These can be time-consuming, with a lot of waiting involved before a clear cause can be found—if one is found at all. This couple faces not only clinical experiences, but emotional ones.

I remember when I was first told that I had endometriosis, in 1983. Once given the diagnosis, I waited for the options he would give me. Maybe taking some specific vitamins would help, or a prescription . . . something I could wrap my arms around. The doctor looked at me and told me that I might as well have a hysterectomy now (at age twenty-three) and get it over with. He continued with, "Nothing living will ever come out of that uterus," delivering the statement in a matter-of-fact tone as he pointed to my stomach. I was devastated. I had only been married for four months, and this was his professional recommendation. He sent me home with the only decision that he offered, which was to call his office with the date that I would like to have the surgery "taken care of."

Although this is an extreme example of how a doctor's-office visit can turn into a life-changing event, many women across the country can relate to the feelings I experienced. It can take several days, even weeks, for them to really grasp what is going on in their own bodies and in their lives. The feelings these women face will be discussed in more detail in the chapters to come. I will tell you now that it is similar to that of accepting death. First there is the disbelief; and then comes the anger; and then the sadness; and then, lastly, the acceptance. Don't misunderstand the acceptance stage of infertility as complacency. You come to a point that you accept that you need to follow another path in order to achieve pregnancy and the birth of your child. You do not, however, accept that your diagnosis is the final answer. The acceptance stage is when you begin to look for options, like those listed earlier in this chapter.

Once a woman is diagnosed, she has several options. With each option comes a monthly cost. Here are three of the most popular options and their average monthly expense.

Clomid (Serophene): a hormone pill that is taken on days 5-9 of the monthly cycle. The average cost is $950 per month, which does not include the actual pills, the injections, ovulation-predictor tests, or pregnancy tests.

FSH (Follicle-stimulating hormone) which is used to evaluate a woman's egg supply and Intrauterine Insemination which is a procedure where the man's sperm are directly inserted into the woman's uterus. This is often used when a man's sperm count is low or a woman has endometriosis: The average cost is $1,815 per month which also does not include the medications or injections.

In-vitro fertilization: The insemination of an extracted and fertilized egg. The average cost is $6,190 per month and does not include medications or embryo storage.

Other options are available, one of which is **Danocrine**. Oral Danocrine is one of the first fertility drugs I was placed on. The purpose of this drug is to stop the growth of the endometriosis. It is similar to testosterone and puts the woman in a state of menopause. Then, once you have been on the drug for a particular time period, and the endometriosis has not had the chance to grow or inhibit any of the reproductive organs, you are taken off the drug with the expectation of regular intercourse (while the coast is clear) and become pregnant before the endometriosis has the opportunity to begin growing again.

When I was placed on Danocrine, my husband and I were told of the odds that I would become pregnant once taken off the drug. Any drug has side effects, and as a woman taking a drug similar to testosterone, I was in for a plethora of them! Strict instructions came with this drug: You must take it at the same time every day. You can take it with or without food, but you must do it the same every time. You can never miss a dose.

Taking Danocrine was kind of like taking care of a gremlin; we always feared the what-ifs. On one occasion, we went away for the weekend, and I left the bag with my Danocrine in it on the table. Once I realized what I had done, we spent the rest of the day running from pharmacy to pharmacy, trying to find one that carried Danocrine so that I would not miss a dose. We were on a time limit: I had to take it by 5:00 p.m. If we had failed, I could have started my period, and we might have had to begin all over again. Endometriosis might have crept in, which meant another laparoscopy and scraping of my uterus so that we had a clean slate to start with again.

Month after month, I took the Danocrine. Every month at the doctor's office, I was told this may be the last month before I could come off it. The drug offered benefits, such as the absence of a period. But then there were the side effects . . . and I suffered more of them every month. First, I dealt with persistent headaches, weight gain, and mood swings. Then came the acne that I had never had before and hair growth in places that I didn't want hair! This was called "masculinization"; I called it "You've got to be kidding!" The most difficult side effect to deal with was the vaginal dryness and irritation. It made intercourse unbearable, even with lubricant. I began crying during intercourse—not out of joy, but out of pain.

After nine months, I was finally taken off the medication. The doctor announced that the fun part could start: trying for that baby we wanted so desperately. Picture, if you will, how excited that made me. There I was, having endured persistent headaches for nine months; I had given up tweezing and begun shaving all the unwanted hair; I was twenty pounds heavier, with a face and even a back full of pimples; emotionally, I felt like Mr. Hyde; and I now had a fear of intercourse due to the painful dryness and irritation. Although some women would be saying "yippee," I envisioned slapping my doctor and spending the next several months on top of the bell tower where I felt I belonged!

Having a general idea of the diagnostic procedures and the most common fertility treatments will help you better comprehend what your loved one has already had to face or will face in this process. A woman or couple has many decisions to make before any fertility process can begin.

CHAPTER THREE

A Day . . . A Week . . . A Month . . . in the Struggle with Infertility

Once a course of treatment is decided upon, a huge change occurs in the regular day-to-day life of a woman undergoing infertility treatments. This chapter will give you an idea of some of those changes and what a "day in the life" looks like.

Few women contemplate infertility until it happens. It comes as a complete surprise. It arrives as an unwanted guest who should have never been allowed to enter your home. There are the apologies to each other for whatever condition is found to be causing the problem. There are the feelings of guilt for ruining the plans that you both had for a family. Infertility feels like an intrusion. It's like being a child again and hearing your mom or dad tell you no to something you want so badly. You are waiting to wake up from a bad dream. You want a phone call from the doctor's office letting you know that a mistake has been made, and there is nothing wrong with you. The most difficult thing to wrap your head around is that you are not in control; it feels as though the infertility is.

As a woman going through infertility, you quickly learn how to talk about and refer to yourself. When you call your doctor's office, you learn to change your usual "Hello, I was calling for . . . " with "This is Lisa Murray, day 5, on day 3 of Clomid." You are known simply as the day of the month of your cycle, and where you are in this month's process. This is not to say that you do not develop a great relationship with your doctor and the amazing nurses that you spend most of your time with.

While my husband, Sean, and I lived in Batesville, Indiana, two nurses, Laurie and Sandy, served as my guardian angels. I don't know how I would have made it through many of the months of the fertility cycle without them. Many times, Laurie held my hand when the injections made me dizzy and nauseated. Sometimes Sandy hugged me when I couldn't stop crying. They also took a minute with me as I stood in front of the bulletin board of "baby success" pictures. Sometimes they would just stand there with me . . . sometimes they would whisper, "Don't worry, your baby's picture will be up there soon."

Even in those moments of compassion, when you are treated by medical staff as a real woman with real feelings, the reality of the matter is that any given facility serves many patients, and time is of the essence . . . so you learn to speak in the fertility code. This makes phone conversations more efficient and helps to save everyone's time.

Now, let's take a look at one whole month together (shown on the next page). This will help you understand what one month of infertility planning looks like and just how much time is spent, how much energy is expended, and how much scheduling takes place. This example of a typical month shows you everything that needs to be planned. This particular month, I chose not to schedule the two days that you would normally have an ultrasound, which would check how well your body is producing eggs. Since the ultrasounds were expensive and not covered by insurance, we chose to have them every other month instead of every month.

Each month is numbered beginning with the first day of your menstrual cycle (which in this month fell on the seventh), which is circled as day one. The word "pill" indicates the days that Clomid was taken. The word "test" indicates when an ovulation-predictor test was taken, and the results of that test are also written in. The words "yes" or "no" indicate whether intercourse took place. The notes in the upper left-hand corner show that in February, Robitussin and baby aspirin were added—the first to thin the cervical mucus to make everything more compatible, and the baby aspirin to . . . well, I don't even remember why. The day of the nineteenth also included the shots in the doctor's office—one in each hip. This was to release the eggs that the Clomid had encouraged my body to produce.

(This is a page from my 1997 pocket calendar. I always kept a separate calendar for my fertility schedule.)

This month is one that I remember quite well. Although it shows on the sixth that I had a negative blood test (pregnancy test), the following day I miscarried due to a faulty attachment (a condition where the fertilized egg does not fully attach to the uterine wall and eventually is expelled by your body). I was at work when I felt as if I had to go to the bathroom. Once there, I had an urge to push, although I didn't feel I needed to have a bowel movement. What did come out was a huge mass of blood and tissue. Upon going to the doctor's the next day, he informed me that between what the blood test results had shown and what I had experienced, I had been about three weeks pregnant. My mom had suffered with several faulty attachments during her childbearing years, so this was not a new term to me.

The miscarriage was somehow both happy and sad for me and my husband. First there was the sadness of loss: asking ourselves "why?" over and over, and "What could I have done differently or done better in order to have carried this baby to full term?" Then there was what the doctor described as "good news": I could get pregnant. This gave us new hope. This meant that the fertility treatments were working. This meant that the crazy month's schedule ahead would be more tolerable this time, because we were one step closer to our child.

Once fertility treatments are in full swing, a couple's lives revolve around their schedule. If you miss a day of the Clomid or start taking it on the wrong day, this could affect the chances of conception. If you do not have the shots on the right day . . . if you do not have intercourse on the right days, or even at the right time of the day . . . anything and everything could affect your chances.

Although I went up for prayer every Sunday at church, and my husband and I prayed together about our future children, there was nothing I wouldn't do (within reason) to conceive a child. Someone told me about agnus-castus, a natural supplement that helps your body to conceive. They insisted I try it and told me of friends of theirs who had tried it successfully. It tasted horrible and made my breath anything but fresh and appealing . . . but I tried it.

Another person told me about "positioning" after intercourse. She told me of one of her friends who conceived after standing on her head for half an hour afterward. So there I was, immediately after intercourse, with my husband standing on the bed holding my legs up so that I could get positioned as comfortably as possible. Then, once sturdy, I stayed there, standing on my head with my back against the headboard and my legs against the wall. To pass the time, if my husband had to go to work (we worked different shifts), he would turn the television on for me. Have you ever watched TV upside down before? After several months of this with no success, I decided that the headaches that followed were not worth it . . . but I had tried it, because this person's friend had tried it and it had worked for them.

Yet another caring individual suggested that pillows were the way to go. After all, her friend was successful in getting pregnant after trying this method. She said that standing on your head didn't cause gravity to pull sperm along the "natural path" and that propping several pillows under my lower back and bottom, with my knees pulled to my chest, would surely do the job. So when intercourse was complete, I would swing my legs over my head (in a very ladylike manner, of course) while my husband would pile several pillows under me. Then I would slowly come to rest on them and stay in this position for at least an hour before moving.

Watching television was out of the question, since all I could see were my knees. (To entertain myself, I would count the beauty marks—I didn't like to call them moles. At that time, I had ten beauty marks on my right knee and seven on my left.) This also became my prayer time—first with my husband holding my hand, and then by myself once I had assured him that I was fine to finish the time alone. Sometimes I would stay like that until I couldn't wait any longer to go to the bathroom. Other times I stopped because I had fallen off the pillows and couldn't get back up.

"Maybe last month I just didn't give it enough time", I would tell myself. "If I could just hold out a little bit longer this time."

Even as a woman of faith, someone who puts her trust and hope in the Lord, I would still try anything (again, within reason) to have the opportunity to give my testimony in church one Sunday morning . . . a testimony I had practiced over and over again. Then, when I finished my testimony, Sean would walk on the platform with our child in his arms, and we would dedicate him or her together. I pictured this day and imagined giving my testimony daily. It lifted me when I was down. It gave me strength to think about dedicating our child back to God.

There was also the part of me who "calls things that are not as though they were" (Romans 4:17, NIV). I tried other women's advice, because after all, God may have put them in my life, at that moment, for a reason: to give me that one suggestion that I had not tried yet! A plaque hanging in our home bears a J. Arnold quote: "Every person God puts into our lives, every experience He gives us, is the perfect preparation for the future that only He can see." I believe that everything happens for a reason, and feeling that faith is believing and doing, I listened to other people's suggestions (which, in retrospect, wasn't always a good idea!)

What is important to understand is that in one month of fertility, a woman goes through what feels like a lifetime of counting, praying, positive thinking, believing, timing, tests, pills, shots, exams, ultrasounds, planned intercourse, emotional ups, emotional downs, and a lot of waiting. Then, if her period starts, there is a time of sadness and a feeling of failure . . . and then it begins all over again. On this day of the month, perhaps she need only take this pill or that pill. On that day of the month, she may spend hours on the phone, in the doctor's office, or both.

Although every day is different, one thing is the same: they are *all* planned. There are appointments, procedures, exams, and blood tests to plan . . . and yes, even intercourse must be planned into the schedule. You are expected to have intercourse every other day (waiting one day in between for the sperm count to rebuild); you are to vary the times of the day (sometimes in the morning and sometimes in the evening); and you are *always* to have intercourse on the day of the injections.

I remember during one of the years of fertility treatments, my husband worked the 3:00 p.m. to 11:00 p.m. shift at a nearby factory, and I was teaching at a local Christian school. On the days that we needed to have intercourse, I would skip lunch and run home. I would have to wake up my husband, who had worked overtime the night before and was currently sound asleep, and inform him that it was "time" . . . and that we needed to hurry, because I had a class soon.

Picture, if you will, just how romantic and spontaneous this scenario is! Women undergoing fertility experience moments like this one regularly. Intercourse can become something that has to be done instead of something that they want to do. Along with putting intercourse into your monthly, weekly, and daily schedule comes more difficulties. Even though you try to make any given encounter as magical as you possibly can, it's hard to forget the reality that it's an obligation. This causes times when it "doesn't" happen. During these times, the pressure on the man can prove overwhelming. Intercourse that has to take place can cause trouble with erections, frustration, anxiety, and at times, not even wanting to try.

Having to perform on demand is not exactly how we picture that magical moment . . . but that is the reality of it when you are on a schedule. As a woman, you sometimes just want to forget about it and rest . . . but you have already put so much time and money into the month that you feel the pressure to have intercourse even when neither of you are up to it. You also live with the possibility, the hope, the belief, that this time could be . . . no, will be. . . the time we conceive.

CHAPTER FOUR

Are You Listening?

Now that you have a general idea of what infertility is and what a couple goes through each month, it is important to ask you this question: Are you listening? Are you *really* listening?

Webster's classifies *listening* as a verb defined as "To make conscious effort to hear. To concentrate on hearing somebody or something. To pay attention to something and take it into account. The act of hearing . . . making an effort to hear something."

When you are with the person in your life who is currently undergoing fertility treatments, are you really listening to her? What I mean is, are you waiting for a lull in the conversation so that you can interject your opinion—your ideas of what you think she should do or try (like standing on their head)—or are you really *making an effort* to hear her?

As many books will tell you, listening takes effort. Listening is a verb, and a verb is an action. So listening is an action! A great way to gauge if you are a good listener is to determine how much of the time you spend listening and how much of the time you spend talking. When someone needs to talk about what they are going through and needs you to just listen to them, keep in mind that a good listener spends 80 percent of the time listening and only 20 percent of the time talking. If you find that your percentage of listening is off, and you are talking more than 20 percent of the time . . . then you are *not* a good listener! Sorry to be the one to burst your bubble of being the perfect friend, but that is the reality.

Part of the effort of listening is controlling your own thoughts. You have to really focus on what the other person is saying in order to avoid mentally making your grocery list while nodding to them. It takes a lot of effort to stop thinking two or three sentences ahead and planning just what you will say in response—all while not really hearing what is currently being said. We get so wrapped up in what we think and feel that we don't really listen to the other person. How many times has your mind wandered as you have been reading this paragraph? Listening and focusing on another person takes effort!

Another question is, have you been practicing active listening? Most people don't. They listen to someone, think they have it all figured out, and then begin to tell the other person just how to fix it. Active listening is the practice of paying close attention to someone and asking questions to ensure that you fully understand. These questions should address feelings: "You sound frustrated. Are you saying . . . ?" or "Since I want to fully understand, it sounds like you are saying . . . [repeat statement from other person] . . . is that what you were saying?Something to keep in mind when you are talking to your friend or family member is just how frustrated he or she may be. Just think about all the commercials on television that are about pregnancy tests, birth control, diapers, ovulation-predictor tests, baby toys, baby food, kids' juice drinks, kids' snacks . . . and the list goes on. Then there are the shows about babies, giving birth, and couples with sixteen kids and counting . . . et cetera, et cetera. People struggling with infertility are bombarded with commercials of women talking about how they don't want children now, and how a product is the perfect birth control for them; movies about teens having children; talk shows about women who didn't even know they were pregnant until they gave birth; storylines with abortions and unwanted pregnancies, and more.

Sometimes—many times—they just want to talk about how they are *feeling.* They want to express their anger, their frustration, and their anxiety—all without being judged, and all without you giving them answers. They just want a caring, listening ear, and possibly a shoulder to cry on. When you and your spouse are talking, and you describe a bad day at work or express frustration with your children, you don't want to hear about how to fix it, what you should have done, or what you should do in the future. You just want to be listened to; you just to be empathized with; you just want to be heard.

I vividly remember one Sunday morning at church. Our pastor asked if anyone needed prayer for themselves or a loved one. One couple stood up and asked for prayer for their niece and her boyfriend. It seems that they had a baby, and during the night, the baby kept crying and crying. The boyfriend had had enough of the baby's cries and decided that the three-month-old needed some discipline. He threw the baby against the wall and solved the problem of listening to the crying. The baby died instantly.

The boyfriend and the couple's niece were facing criminal charges and needed prayer. I felt such a swell of emotions rise within me. I stood up and walked out of the sanctuary, and then out of the door. Sometime later, my husband found me sitting on a picnic table on the side of the church, crying uncontrollably. I just kept yelling, "Why? Why? Why were they able to have this child . . . this child that they murdered . . . while we are still struggling? Why?"

This was one of those times when I really didn't want an answer from Sean . . . I wanted one from God. I didn't want to hear any rationalizing from Sean or how "these things just happen sometimes." I just wanted him to listen and let me get out my anger and frustration. He put his arm around me, handed me a Kleenex, and just kept saying, "I don't know."

At many points in the infertility journey, your friend just wants you to listen. She may just need your arm around her as she cries. She may just need you to sit there with her quietly and not say a word. She may need someone to pray for her when she is struggling. A friend like that is indeed rare.

Listening and friendship are discussed many times in the Bible. Here are just a few verses that are close to my heart:

"Let the wise listen and add to their learning." (Proverbs 1:5 NIV)

"A friend loves at all times . . . " (Proverbs 17:17 NIV)

"Do not forsake your friend and the friend of your father . . . " (Proverbs 27:10 NIV)

"A time to be silent and a time to speak . . . " (Ecclesiastes 3:7)

"He who answers before listening—that is his folly and his shame." (Proverbs 18:13 NIV)

"Everyone should be quick to listen, slow to speak and slow to become angry . . . " (James 1:19 NIV)

So you need to ask yourself, "Am I quick to listen . . . or am I quick to give my opinion?"

CHAPTER FIVE

What *Not to* Say

Now that you understand how important it is to listen, let's talk about what isn't beneficial when it is time to talk. As I have traveled throughout the country, both as a motivational speaker and as a woman in retail, I have talked to many women. The topic that comes up the most is infertility. No matter what city or state I am in, women who are having a difficult time conceiving seem to find me. Certainly God plays a major role in this. He knows that my experiences can be beneficial to other women who are now in the same shoes that I walked in. He also knows that although their circumstances might be different, I really can relate to what they are going through.

Through the conversations with these women and through my own experience, I have learned of several recurring comments that women struggling with infertility find unhelpful. I will now share with you some of the most frequent comments that are unhelpful and even frustrating to hear—comments that most people seem to feel the need to make to a woman going through infertility treatments.

➤ "Just relax." Really? Did you see the monthly schedule? That schedule is just for Clomid treatments! Your friend already knows the value of relaxing and has heard this statement many times from her doctor. This piece of advice would fall into the "frustrating" category. It is always easy for someone to tell someone else to relax. It is kind of like when you are about to have the metal speculum inserted during your Pap smear, and your doctor says "Just relax!" We know we need to . . . but the reality of it is, "You've got to be kidding!"

➤ "Try not to think about it." This seems to be another common piece of advice that friends give, and it is about as effective as telling them to relax. Again, when you are following a specific and detailed schedule, it is almost impossible *not* to think about treatment. It is also interesting to note that babies and children are the topic of most people's conversations. Think about it the next time you are sitting in a restaurant or at church, shopping or at the grocery store: almost everyone is talking about their child or someone else's. Take some time and just listen, like we talked about in the previous chapter. Then try to imagine what a woman who is struggling to have a child hears and how it makes her feel.

➤ "Remember Sarah." Most women are familiar with and have read the story of Sarah and Abraham in Genesis, chapters 15-23. Sure, the story is inspiring and shows the amazing love and faithfulness of God and all that He is able to do through those that are called. This story, however, is not always one a woman who is trying to conceive wants to hear. When women are struggling with the reality that beginning their family is taking a lot longer than they imagined, they are not encouraged to hear about a woman who had her first child at the age of ninety! Although Sarah lived to be one hundred and twenty-seven, she only was able to be with her firstborn son, Isaac, for thirty-seven years of his life. Every woman who is struggling with conception is acutely aware of the average lifespan. With thoughts like, "If I have our child now, I will be this old when they start school, and this old when they start to drive, and this old when they graduate from high school." The passage of time, the ticking of their biological clock, and the continuing advances in their age: such measurements are always in the back of these women's minds. They really don't need someone reminding them of what they are already thinking about . . . and already worrying about.

Women undergoing fertility treatments are aware that the infertility rate rises as their age increases, as seen below:

- ➢ Ages 15-29: infertility is at 11%
- ➢ Ages 30-34: infertility is at 16.9%
- ➢ Ages 35-39: infertility is at 22.6%
- ➢ Ages 40-44: infertility rises to 27.4%

My sister, Delyse, had a "miracle baby" at the age of forty-four. Her son, Travis, is now eight, and my sister is fifty-two. When Travis was born, Delyse had already figured out all the ages that she would be at the monumental times in Travis's life. By the time my nephew is forty years old, my sister will be eighty-four. Women are always multitasking; along with multitasking comes multithinking. Women are always thinking about many things at once. This means they are always aware of . . . well . . . everything.

> "I understand." Although your friend or family member desperately needs you to listen to what she is going through, and be there for her, she does not need you to tell her that you understand what she is going through. If you want to be helpful, don't pretend to understand or say that you understand what your friend is going through . . . because if you have children—even one—the reality is that you don't. Empathy is described as the capacity to, through imagination rather than literally, share the sadness or happiness of another sentient being. It can be very helpful to let her know that you understand that she is sad or frustrated. But it can be very upsetting to tell her that you understand what she is going through. It is no different than telling someone who has just lost his or her mother or father that you understand how they feel when your parents are both living.

> "On a day like today . . . I'd give you one of my kids." Nothing is more frustrating to a woman struggling to conceive than hearing comments from people who do not seem to appreciate what they have. When you are desiring a child of your own so badly that you feel you will just lie down and die if it doesn't happen, hearing a woman make any kind of comment similar to the one above is really just plain insulting. No matter how innocently it is intended, it is not funny and should be avoided like the plague!

> The last thing a woman wants or needs when struggling with fertility is pity. You can see it in people's faces. You can feel it when they avoid you because they don't know what to say to you. Just be yourself and treat her as you normally would.

> Do not speak prophetically into her life. Don't get me wrong: I *know* that God speaks to people, and I believe in the spiritual gifts. What I want to stress is that you must know for sure that God is telling you to share something with a woman who is struggling with fertility. Otherwise you are doing harm, not good. If I actually bore all of the children that other women have spoken into my life, I would be like the old woman who lived in a shoe—I would have so many children that I wouldn't know what to

do! Women are compassionate by nature. They want to help. They pray, and sometimes their wishful thinking results in telling a woman who is desperate for a word, "Thus saith the Lord." I was told that we would have twins, not once, but twice. We were told what the names of our children would be. One woman told me that she saw me leaning over a bassinet, taking care of my baby. Another woman saw me giving my testimony on a Sunday morning. Here is an excerpt from my journal of yet another prophetic word from a well-meaning friend.

July 31, 1998

Eileen [not her real name] came to see if I wanted to go for a walk. Today was my first adjustment with Dr. Trisha, and she told me to walk a lot. Hopefully the adjustments will help with getting pregnant. I had all but decided not to walk today, and then came a knock at the door. Eileen told me God wants to bless us with a child, and by this time next year, we would have a child of our own! She said that God wants us to know that we are here for a reason, and God is using us here, and He has a great plan for us, but we need to be patient. She also told me that God has seen me cry and heard my calls to Him, and He wants to hold me in His arms . . . that when we hurt, He hurts with us. Eileen said I needed to spend time alone in God's presence and get to know God more intimately—that I had one year before I would have a baby and not have time to myself anymore.

One year and much prayer later . . . we were still longing for a child.

This is just one example of a woman with the best intentions wanting to speak encouragement into my life. The problem comes when these women really have not heard from God. They want so much to be used as an encourager that they speak what *they* are feeling and not what God is saying. Fortunately I have a strong enough relationship with God that I did not rely on what other people spoke into my life. If I had, think of how devastated I could have been when this timeline expired and I still had no baby! I could have ended up bitter, angry at God, angry at Eileen, and even more discouraged.

This is why it is so important that when you want to encourage a woman struggling with conception, you are careful in how you choose to do it. I cannot caution you enough to *not* add God's name to what you have to say unless you know that you have heard from God. And remember, your statement should be a *confirmation* of what God has already spoken to her first.

Even with the best intentions, the comments mentioned will only bring frustration, a little aggravation, and sometimes impatience toward the deliverer of the comment. This is especially true if the woman has heard these comments before . . . and trust me, she will have heard them before. It is kind of like when your dentist drills your teeth, and as you touch the spot with your tongue, you say, "Wow, it feels like the Grand Canyon!" Having worked as a dental assistant for eight years, I can tell you that this comparison is made approximately six times a day. Of course, you think you are the first person to think of this clever analogy and, ready or not, out comes the comment.

This chapter follows the previous chapter on listening so that you hopefully will begin to listen more . . . and avoid comments like these. If we all begin to practice James 1:19 more—being slow to speak and quick to listen—I'm sure we could have all avoided things that we have regretted saying. The good news is that you can help, And the chapters ahead will tell you how.

CHAPTER SIX

What About Adoption?

Although several comments about adoption could be included in the previous chapter, I believe this topic deserves a chapter all its own. Why? Adoption is such a personal decision made between a man and wife that it should be tread upon very lightly.

➤ The first, most common question that people ask a woman or couple having trouble having children is, "Have you thought about adoption?" Again, I know that this is commonly said with the best intentions, but let me share some of the thoughts that women have discussed with me regarding how they felt after being asked this question.

"Do you think I crawled out from under a rock yesterday?"

"Duh, what is adoption?"

"Do they think we are stupid?"

"That's easy to ask when they already have children of their own."

"Adoption is always an option, but I want to feel our child grow inside of me. Don't they understand that?"

"Am I supposed to feel selfish for wanting a child of my own?"

➤ The second adoption statement I want to discuss is one of my personal favorites: "You should just adopt. One of my friends did, and as soon as they adopted, she got pregnant."

On a personal note: If I had a dollar for every time my husband or I heard this statement, we would have been able to retire years ago. And if every person who made this statement really knew someone who this happened to . . . I would think that the population would be doubled! Don't get me wrong: I'm sure that this has happened to many people. But I believe that many people who make this statement heard the story from a friend of a friend of a friend, or maybe just heard the story somewhere. Whatever you share with someone, make sure that it is firsthand knowledge, not something you read or heard "somewhere."

➤ A third common statement is, "You should adopt. It is *easy* nowadays."

Let me share with you some of the average adoption costs today. Keep in mind that these costs do not include medical expenses for the child, medical expenses for the birth mother, living expenses, legal representation, counseling, and any travel expenses.

1. Domestic public-agency adoption: Approx. $2,500

2. Domestic private adoption:
   $4,000 to $30,000+

3. Domestic independent adoption:
   $8,000 to $30,000+

4. Intercountry private agency: $7,000 to $25,000
   (also does not include escorting fees, child foster
   care, parent travel, and in-country stay)

My husband, Sean, and I tried adopting several times. Once, we came so close that we were packing for the trip to Colorado to pick up our son. We were currently the youth pastors at our church, and we had let the entire district know of our desire to adopt a baby or toddler. Following service one Sunday, our senior pastor's wife called us into the boardroom and sat us down. We weren't sure what was going on. She looked at us with tears in her eyes. I began to cry and wasn't even sure why.

She finally composed herself and told us of a family in Colorado. A woman from her church had talked to her pastor and told him about her nephew (I'll call him Aaron), who had been mistreated by her sister. He had been left in a crib for his entire short life of nine months. He had developed a flat spot on the back of his head from not being picked up or moved. He was covered in diaper rash from not having his diapers changed regularly, averaging once per day. Her sister, she explained, had been picked up for drugs many times and was not interested in taking care of her son. She had already given up three other children to foster care, and now it was Aaron's turn.

Aaron was undernourished, forgotten, and uncared for. Our hearts melted. Both Sean and I were crying and asking, "What can we do?" The sister had been told about Sean and me and wanted to talk to us. We set up a time and talked to her for over two hours. We agreed to background checks, and references were sent off. Aaron's aunt met with the rest of the family members, and they all agreed that since we didn't have any children of our own, Aaron would be well loved and cared for. She called us with the great news.

Sean and I were ecstatic! We received pictures and sent them to all of our family members in Michigan and all our friends and church family in Indiana. We went shopping, thanked God, and thanked our pastors.

There was only the final court hearing. Aaron's aunt said it was just a formality. The foster family that Aaron had been placed with already had thirteen children that they had adopted, and they were in their late fifties. Aaron's aunt was going to be there on Aaron's behalf to let the judge know of the family's decision and give him our information. Then we would fly out the next day to hold him in our arms and take him home.

At the end of the hearing, the judge turned to the foster family and asked one final question: "Since Aaron has been through so much already, would you consider adopting him so that he doesn't have to be moved again?"

Much to the surprise of Aaron's biological family, the foster family said, "Sure, okay, we can keep him." The judge slammed down his gavel, and that was that. We received the phone call that afternoon: the judge's mind could not be changed, especially since the foster parents had agreed to keep him.

Needless to say, Sean and I were devastated. I remember crying with his picture in my hand for hours. I had had to let go of the promise of a child every month, when my period began . . . and now I had to let go of an actual child—a baby who needed us, and whom we already loved.

This was the first of several attempts at adoption. Another mother changed her mind at the hospital after the baby was born. We were heartbroken again. There are only so many times a couple can go through the adoption process with unsuccessful outcomes. There is only so much of your heart you can keep giving away without it becoming empty or permanently broken.

Adoption is a very delicate subject and should not be just thrown out there, as one would suggest a place to eat after church on a Sunday morning. It should be discussed only with close friends and family members when they initiate the subject. One way to let them know that you are there for them if you think this may be an option is to simply say, "Whatever you two decide, we just want you to know that if you are considering adoption, we would be happy to be a reference for you if you need us to." This opens the door to discussion, lets them know that you care, and also lets them know that you are there for them.

CHAPTER SEVEN

How to Be Helpful

Proverbs 18:21 tells us that "the tongue has the power of life and death, and those who love it will eat its fruit." Everyone worries about saying the right thing to someone who is going through something difficult. Sometimes it is not what you *do* say, but what you *don't* say that can make a difference.

My friend, Rachel, and I had been going up for prayer at church for a few years. Eventually Rachel got pregnant and had her first child, a son. Rachel and her husband, Jeff, named him Miles. Sean and I were so happy for them. We love Miles and we were equally excited when Rachel and Jeff learned they were expecting their second child.

We lived next door to them at the time and loved being part of their lives. Month after month, as I continued to struggle with infertility, it became more and more difficult to spend time with them as a family. I know that my being upset was due to my struggle, but understanding that didn't make the feeling any easier to endure. I will never forget what Rachel said to me one day. She took my hands and looked me in the eyes and said, "Lisa, I have to be honest. I cannot stand here and tell you that I understand how you feel anymore. We used to go up for prayer together, and we were in the same boat. Now I have two children, and to be honest . . . I can't remember what it felt like to want children and not be able to have them. I just want you to know that I am here for you, and I will help you in any way possible."

Wow . . . how refreshing: someone who was not afraid to tell me that she *didn't* understand what I was going through! So many people had told me that they understood, while I knew they couldn't possibly understand. Finally, someone had been straight with me; I have never forgotten how much that meant to me.

Proverbs 12:18 says, "Reckless words pierce like a sword, but the tongue of the wise brings healing." When we speak without thinking, we are being reckless, and the result is not productive. If we are wise with our words, they bring healing to the heart and the soul. Sometimes help comes in a different package.

Hoping for a child can involve a lot of prayer. With prayer comes repentance. We ask for forgiveness for all of our wrongs so that nothing stands in the way of our prayer. We try not to let doubt creep in, because that may mean our faith is not strong enough.

We practice Romans 4:17, which tell us to "Call things that are not as though they were." So we thank God for our unborn children, describing them, naming them, praying for their lives and future spouses. We talk about how many children we desire, whether we want a boy or girl, a blonde or a brunette, and we even list their talents. There are books on supernatural pregnancies and how to achieve them. Sometimes all the believing and faith and certainty month after month can take its toll on even those with the strongest faith.

One Sunday after service, Valarie, an amazing prayer warrior and friend, walked up to me and said, "Lisa, you look tired. How about you just take this week off, and I will believe for you?" That's all she said—one simple sentence—yet it changed my whole countenance. It felt like a huge weight had been lifted off my shoulders. I knew that she would intercede for me, pray for me, and believe for me, so that I could . . . for a lack of better words . . . take a break. What an amazing woman and friend!

Another way to help is to just simply ask, "What can I do for you?" This is what my friend Angie asked me whenever she saw me struggling. She didn't try to give me any answers. She didn't try to tell me what to do or tell me what she thought I should do. She simply would ask me, "What do you need from me?"

Here are some other suggestions based on what my family, Angie, Rachel, Nola and Val did for me!

- ⊥ Make her smile.
- ⊥ Give her a shoulder to cry on.
- ⊥ Sit there quietly while neither of you say anything.
- ⊥ Make chocolate-chip cookies.
- ⊥ Sympathize when hormones get the best of her.

⊥ Send her a card in the mail for no reason.

⊥ Never say "I understand."

⊥ Don't tell her what to do.

⊥ Help her snap out of her "down" times.

⊥ Make her a music CD with all your favorite songs.

⊥ Make her something that tells her that you are believing with her: Val made us a baby blanket that was so beautiful. We still have it so that we can bless Lindsay or Travis with it some day (if they choose to have a family of their own).

⊥ Send her a friendship card on Mother's Day. Sean still gives me a "Happy Mother's Day" card from our dogs and signs it with paw prints.

⊥ Go for a walk together.

⊥ Just listen.

⊥ Be sensitive to the fact that Mother's Day and Father's Day can be extremely difficult days for couples struggling to conceive.

CHAPTER EIGHT

Other Issues
That May Arise

Other conditions come along with infertility that are rarely talked about but important to know in order to better empathize with your friend/ relative. Women going through infertility treatments are more likely to suffer from one or more of the following:

1. **Depression:** It is hard to keep your hopes high and to think positive month after month. With every menstrual cycle comes the feeling of failure, hopelessness, and great sadness. It is also important to note that sometimes, when we are "listening," we tend to tell someone that they "shouldn't feel that way." In the attempt to help someone feel better or think differently, we make matters worse by telling the person that his or her feelings are not valid. This is done through comments that are said with the best intentions, but actually tell the person to just change the way they feel.

2-17-03

Big snow and ice storm—no church yesterday a.m. or p.m. No work today—everything is closed. Supposed to warm up a little tomorrow, so it will probably all melt. Leaving for Michigan on Friday. Plane for Grand Cayman leaves Saturday a.m. Wish I were looking forward to it. Sean and I are not getting along . . . haven't spoken much for two days. Getting snowed in should be fun; this wasn't. Tired of feeling unwanted and undesirable. Having trouble praying. This Wednesday is the last night for us as the youth pastors. We should be doing great and getting relaxed and "doing our hobby," as people refer to trying to get pregnant . . . but we are not, and we're not. Sean is sick again. I'm just not happy. God, help me keep a good head . . . ready to give up on everything. I feel fat and ugly, and I don't have the energy to do anything about it.

This is just one entry about how I was feeling during a month of fertility treatments. Between the hormone medications, the schedule, and all the emotions, a battle with depression is always waiting in the wings.

When having intercourse changes from "making love" to "having sex" . . . let's just say that you could sometimes quote an old song: "the thrill is gone/ there's no desire/girl, we've got to feed the fire . . . " Both my husband and I went through times of feeling undesirable because everything seemed so difficult at times. The hormones made me feel fat, bloated, ugly, sad, tired . . . tired . . . and tired.

Although not every woman goes through this, many do. Sometimes just talking it out with someone who will listen can make the difference. No one can make you feel different, but talking it out and voicing your frustration out loud to someone who cares can help alleviate the bad feelings and help you feel better. It is kind of like having a good cry when you need one.

> No one feels comfortable discussing their trouble in the bedroom. It is also difficult to talk about how the trouble in the bedroom makes you feel. But the reality is . . . it is reality. The stress of a man having to perform can cause the desire to avoid intercourse altogether. The avoidance can cause the woman to feel undesirable. Feeling that your husband does not desire you can cause more stress in the relationship and more feelings of inadequacy for both the man and the woman. Add the fact that the date tells you that it *has* to happen or the whole month of prescriptions, tests, and injections were for nothing . . . let's just say that candles and soft music don't always do the trick!

2. **Anxiety:** Look again at a typical month—enough said.

3. At times, she can also feel **panic or experience paranoia.** Hormones play a role, and so does the overwhelming desire to conceive.

4. **Stress:** You need to relax, but you can't. You want your schedule to go smoothly, but life always throws you a curveball. You set time aside to be together, but things happen. Through all of the fertility schedules and treatments, life is still going on.

5. **Social phobia**: It becomes more and more difficult to attend events like baby showers, family reunions, weddings, church on Mother's Day, and any Mother's Day celebration. Visiting someone with a newborn is also very hard. These events can sometimes cause the anxiety, stress, and depression described previously.

If your friend or relative declines to attend an event, it is important to not take it personally. This is a time to simply ask, "What can I do for you?" They may need you to take their card/present for them to the event. They may need to talk through what they are feeling, because even they do not understand why they feel the need to avoid the gathering. Again, this is a great time to practice active listening.

There was a time period of about six years during which I could not even think about attending a baby shower. Just entering a baby store or infant department would be enough to give me an anxiety attack. I didn't want to feel this way. I wanted to be able to be happy for my friends who were having children (and I really was happy for them), but I could not face them, the showers, or the other guests. It felt like all eyes were looking at me, thinking, "Oh, that poor girl . . . she still hasn't gotten pregnant."

My anxiety even caused me to avoid my friendship with Rachel, mentioned in an earlier chapter, for years. It was not that I didn't love her or care for her, or that I was not happy for her . . . I just couldn't emotionally face her. My emotions were so mixed. I felt anger and frustration with every baby commercial. I grew tired of all the "teen mom" movies. I saw pregnant women everywhere I went and wanted to scream.

Fortunately for me, Rachel understood. She told me that she was there for me and to do whatever I needed to make things easier for myself during this difficult time in my life. Because of how compassionate she was, we are still friends today. I am now able to enjoy her and her three children because she gave me the time I needed to deal with my feelings. She allowed me time to heal. She prayed for me. And not ever . . . not even once . . . did she tell me how I should feel or what I should think.

CHAPTER NINE

A Reminder to You Who Are Struggling with Infertility

Although people will sometimes say things that will hurt your feelings, upset you, and even anger you . . . remember that they don't do it intentionally. Sometimes people just don't know what to say, and many times they don't think before they say something.

I was standing outside my office at our church one Sunday morning, waiting for Sean to finish up in the sanctuary. As I waited for him, I began a conversation with our pastor's wife. She was telling me about a friend of hers who was having a difficult time conceiving a second child. As I stood there listening, she continued to tell me about everything that this woman and her husband had been going through. It always seemed as if anyone who knew anyone having a difficult time getting pregnant felt the need to talk to me about it. Then she continued the conversation with, "I just don't understand what she is thinking. I mean, she is forty years old. Doesn't she stop to think about how silly it is to be trying to have a child at that age? Even if she gets pregnant now, she will be almost fifty-seven years old when her child gets their driver's license." Just as quickly as the words flew out of her mouth, her eyes met mine. I could see her mind reeling as her face began to turn white. Her face turned from an expression of disgust with her friend to one of mortification at what she had just said. I was, after all, forty-two at the time and still going through fertility treatments. As she put her hand to her mouth and began to look for the words to apologize, I stopped her. I reassured her that I didn't take it personally and understood that a lot of people think it is strange to still be trying for a child at my age. She breathed a sigh of relief as I touched her shoulder to let her know that there were no hard feelings.

Sometimes, no matter how much someone cares about you, they can still say the wrong thing. Anyone who has been married for any length of time can attest to that. Consider the old business saying "It's nothing personal—it's just business." You need to remember that when someone says something offensive, "It's nothing personal—it's just ignorance." If you can just remember this and repeat it to yourself every time you are facing a situation like the one above, you can make it through any conversation, no matter how difficult it may be.

Here are some other ways I dealt with awkward situations:

! When someone said something really ridiculous to me, forgive me, Lord, but I would picture myself slapping them silly. I began to refer to this feeling as "the spirit of slap" coming over me. This helped to make me smile and walk away instead of actually following through with what I was thinking.

! If I felt my blood pressure rising, I would excuse myself with, "Sorry, I need to use the restroom."

If possible, I would just exit through a different door.

! Educating someone is always an option. This just depends on where your emotions and hormone levels are at the time. It also depends on how receptive you feel that person will be. I found that with everything else I was facing daily, I would save my energy if I thought it would be wasted.

! One of my favorites was to just change the subject to them. Somehow, if I answered their questions or comments with a question about their lives, I was home free. Since I felt comfortable discussing my feelings and progress with very few people, asking a question was an easy way for me to switch the subject. I never wanted to hurt anyone's feelings by telling them that it was none of their business or that I didn't want to talk about it. With a question, I was showing concern for them, and they were happy to talk about themselves. Keep in mind that I was not being insincere; I was just doing what I needed to in order to feel at peace with myself and with them.

! When everything within me wanted to say things like "Duh! Are you really that stupid? . . . Do I look that stupid to you? . . . What are you thinking? . . . It's a good thing you don't know what I am thinking! . . . Do you even know what you are talking about?" and other equally lovely thoughts,

I would just say, "As soon as we know something, you will be the first to know." Then I would quickly walk away. Spending too much time with a person who is causing those thoughts doesn't do anyone any good. If you have something ready to say that can stop the conversation and help you leave at the same time, it will save you a lot of frustration. With your emotions on edge and your hormones going berserk on a daily basis, you sometimes need to choose your battles. It isn't healthy or helpful to you (especially since you are supposed to "relax" and "try not to think about it") to stay in situations that only cause you added stress.

Also, remember how important it is for you to find a stress reliever that works for you.

- ♥ Take long walks.
- ♥ Touch base daily with a family member who gets you.
- ♥ Talk to a close friend.
- ♥ Keep a journal.
- ♥ Get lost in a movie with your husband.
- ♥ Spoil your pets.
- ♥ Find a hobby that makes you feel good. Mine were photography and pottery.
- ♥ Listen to motivational CDs (to remind you that there is nothing wrong with you).
- ♥ Spoil yourself with a pedicure, massage, or facial.

♥ Take a day off . . . from everything. Just splib (our family's word for doing nothing) on the couch and watch old movies or shows you've recorded. Don't even get out of your jammies! Caution: this can become addictive and needs to be monitored so it does not become a regular habit!

♥ Sing to yourself (I always sang to God and thanked Him for everything that I *did* have as I longed for what I did *not* have). It can become easy to only remember what you do not currently have (a child) and not remember what you do have (your health, family, home, job, husband, clothes, food, and so on).

♥ Schedule regular date nights with your honey. Keep each time together interesting by trying new restaurants neither of you have ever been to.

♥ Do something different together, like going bowling. Mixing things up keeps your mind from always being focused on fertility.

CHAPTER TEN

What Happens if it Doesn't Happen?

June 15, 1999

My Sunday school teacher asked us to write down our passions a few weeks ago. He said to write down not what we feel our gifts from God are, but what our passions are.

Here is the first entry on my list:

1. Wanting to be a mom. To feel a child growing inside of me. To look upon the face of a miracle that is part Sean and part me. To have our own family!

At the time of this entry, I had already been trying to conceive a child for over a decade. I had practiced the testimony that I would give to our congregation over and over again, day after day. It kept me going; it kept me motivated. I had also read many books on childbirth and Biblical children's names. Sean and I had picked out names for the three children we desired.

One of the books discussed how you should thank God in detail for your future children, thanking Him for their perfect vision, their specific personalities, their talents, their future spouses . . . everything. We had prayed about our children so many times that they already felt real.

In December 2003, my doctor told me that it was time for a hysterectomy. I had just had a blood transfusion because my blood and iron levels were so low. Many endometriomas had reformed, and my endometriosis was once again attaching my uterus to my bowels and bladder. All the facts told me that I should go through the hysterectomy, and my body was clearly ready . . . but my emotions were not.

I wasn't ready to let go of Lydia Elizabeth, who would be named after my two sisters, Delyse (whom we call Dee) and Hily, along with Hily's daughter, Lindsay Elizabeth. Lydia would be smart, with big blue eyes and sandy blonde hair. The second born, Daniel Thomas, would be named after Sean's friend Dan, who had died several years earlier, and Sean's father, Thomas, who had also died several years ago. Daniel would be very creative, with hazel eyes and curly, light-brown hair. Then there was Maria Lynn, named after my Grandma Kujawski and my mom. Maria would have a big heart and great sense of humor. She would be that fireball who always lit up a room whenever she entered it.

I wasn't ready to let go of our children. One more surgery just might make the difference and put us on track with our family. I chose to have surgery to remove the endometriomas and have the endometriosis scraped from my uterus, bladder, and bowels one more time.

For a woman facing the possibility of not having her own biological children, there is no objective way to specify when the right time to end fertility treatments will be. Every woman must make that decision on her own . . . when *she* is ready. Although my husband knew that I should have had the hysterectomy in 2003 for the sake of my health, he stood by my decision to wait. He knew, as I did, that I was not ready to quit. I was not ready to say good-bye to Lydia, Danny, and Maria.

After the surgery, we went to Michigan to visit our family for Christmas and for me to recover. This surgery could not be performed through a laparoscope; it required an incision from hip to hip in order to remove all of the cysts and clean up my uterine area. It wasn't long before I knew I had made the wrong decision.

Christmas consisted of me spending most of my time in the bathroom and almost needing another transfusion. As embarrassing as it was, I even needed to borrow some of my nephew Travis's diapers in order be able to sleep more than two hours at a time. I ended up needing to see a hematologist in order to get my blood levels healthy enough to continue fertility treatments. Even with the many trips to the hematologist and dealing with the blood loss each month, I don't think I could have made any other decision. I was not ready yet, and nothing could change that.

Some women I have spoken to over the years dealt with feelings that surfaced during infertility treatment—the sort of feelings that I believe are the most difficult to face. These feelings are not only difficult for the woman who is experiencing them, but for her husband and family as well. The women who feel them also feel the need to talk about them, yet husbands and family members find such feelings extremely hard to discuss and understand. Here are several feelings that I experienced throughout the process, and sometimes still feel today:

♥ There is a feeling of failure as a wife. No matter how much my husband reassured me that he did not marry me just so that I could supply him with children, I still suffered with a very strong feeling of failure. After all, the next step after getting married is to have children. To build a family. To create and enjoy family traditions and special family events together. To celebrate Mother's Day and Father's Day as new parents. To get that "Baby's First Christmas" ornament for the tree. To decide just how I would share the happy news with my spouse.

♥ There is a feeling of failure as a daughter/daughter-in-law. Knowing how happy My Mother and in-laws would be when we shared with them that they would be grandparents, and knowing that this would never be possible, feels like failure. I wanted to shop for all the picture frames that say "Our Grandchild" and all the cards that say "To Grandma and Grandpa." I wanted to attend family get-togethers to share your bundle of joy with sisters, brothers, parents, aunts, and uncles. I wanted to decide just how we would share the happy news with our parents.

♥ There is a feeling of failure as a woman. No matter how many attributes your husband or friend tells you that you have, it does not take the place of the ability to be a mom. After all, as women we were made to be able to produce life. The miracle of conception is reserved for women, along with the feeling of your unborn child growing inside of you, feeling them kick, holding your husband's hand on your stomach as you share those magical moments, and the amazement of nursing your baby. As a woman, you long to watch your children grow up, take their first steps, and speak their first words. As a woman, you were created to give birth. Failing to conceive feels like failing as a woman.

No matter how difficult it is for others to understand these feelings of failure, they are very real. It is important not to dismiss them or downplay how strong they can be. It is imperative that you really listen and let these feelings be expressed. Just as people who lose a loved one need to express their anger, ask all the "what if" questions, and talk about their last days with that loved one over and over again in order to begin the healing process, so must a woman who is unable to have children of her own be allowed to express the feeling of failure and loss in order for the healing to begin.

Once it is clear that conception is not a possibility, acceptance takes time.

Deciding to schedule my complete hysterectomy on November 9, 2004, as mentioned in the first chapter, was the most difficult choice that I have ever made. What may seem as simple as scheduling time off work and as practical as doing what is best for my body was anything but.

The feelings of failure were overwhelming.

I apologized to my husband for not being able to give us a family. I apologized for him not ever being able to put his hand on my belly and feel his child move. He would never be able to look into the face of his son or daughter and kiss him or her on the forehead. He would never hear the word "Daddy."

I apologized to my mother-in-law for not being able to give her a grandchild. She would never know what her son's child would look like or sound like. She would not have the opportunity to take pictures and videos to share with her friends. She would never receive a birthday card from our child to "Grandma."

Although my sister Hily had a daughter, and my sister Delyse had a son, I still felt I had failed at giving my mom another grandchild. I had practiced how I would tell her I was pregnant so many times. Sean and I would talk about it and get excited at the prospect of when that time came. We had decided we would break the news of our pregnancy by giving her a photo frame that said "Grandma's Angels" with space for three pictures. Then we would just smile as she pondered the three frame holes, since she currently had two grandchildren.

Then there was the most difficult of all . . .

Before going to the hospital for surgery, I had to say goodbye to our children. Although they had never been born, I still felt the loss of ever knowing them. I had to let go of the dream of Lydia Elizabeth and her big blue eyes. I had to say good-bye to Danny and how much I just knew he would resemble his Grandpa Bud, who had died on Christmas Eve in 1985. Then there was Maria, who would have been our free spirit. Having my uterus removed from my body was like having them removed from our lives. I mourned for them. I mourned for my husband. I mourned for myself.

When I arrived at the hospital, I already had arranged for an immediate sedative injection into my IV. I knew that I would have second thoughts, a lot of anxiety, overwhelming sadness, and the feeling of wanting to run and never look back. The surgery took longer than expected. My uterus was heavy and blood soaked, like a large sponge, and had to be removed in four sections. The hysterectomy had to be complete, removing ovaries and all, since the endometriosis had spread throughout my abdomen.

CHAPTER ELEVEN

Life After Loss

Whether a woman ends up unable to have children of her own due to a hysterectomy, an illness, a defect, cancer, or a host of many other causes, the loss is still just that: loss. A woman must then find life after the loss.

After a death in the family, many times people stop talking about the person who has passed away. Sometimes it is out of sadness, and sometimes it is out of not wanting to upset anyone else. The healing comes from being able to talk about the loss of a loved one. This is also when acceptance begins, and life can go on. The finality of a woman knowing that she will never have a child of her own is the same. For healing to begin, she must be allowed to talk about it. The more the subject is avoided, the more difficult it is to move on.

There are also times when loved ones want to just blow a loss off as "no big deal" not out of lack of caring, but out of not wanting to upset anyone. Please remember that it really *is* a big deal to those who are experiencing it, and downplaying its importance can be very harmful.

If the bad news is that the fertility battle has ended with another negative pregnancy test, the good news is that you can help your loved one through it. The fertility journey is extremely difficult, but the finality of it being over and unsuccessful is extremely traumatic in a woman's life.

When I woke up from my surgery, I felt the tears roll down the sides of my face. Although I was in a lot of pain, my tears were not caused by the many staples across my stomach. They were tears of loss. They were tears of sadness, tears of embarrassment, and tears of failure, but mostly, they were tears of loss.

I am sharing what I experienced and how I felt in order to help you understand how your loved one may be feeling. Please remember that everyone is different and will be affected in different ways. For me, writing down how the finality of not having children affected me is extremely difficult. The reason I am sharing this with you now is so I can tell you how I have managed to live life after loss.

Since I required an incision, once again, from hip to hip, I was in the hospital for three days. During that time, I found it difficult to look people in the eye; I didn't want them to know what I had been through. Those who remembered me from previous surgeries looked at me with that look of pity. Others just made what they thought were funny comments about not having to deal with having a period anymore.

Once I got home, I felt lost. I had focused on fertility for so long, I wasn't sure what to do now. I wasn't even sure who I was anymore. I was dealing with feelings of failure. I felt such a tremendous loss and sadness. I also felt something

that I hadn't been expecting: I felt ashamed. I felt I had
let so many people down. I somehow even felt that I let
God down.

I began to pray for strength and direction. I believe that
everything happens for a reason, and I knew there must be
a reason why I had been unable to have children. I prayed
for God to use me to help other women, and He has been
faithful, as always. It seemed that every church I minister
in and every place I travel for work, women talk to me
about their fertility problems. When I speak at women's
conferences or church groups, I am always asked to pray
for women who had been unable to conceive. When I pray
for them I can feel their pain and sense their longing. I am
able to relate to them on a very personal level. This has
given my journey new direction. I previously had my life
laid out differently, but God had another plan. God has
given my "'life after loss" new meaning and a purpose.

Sometimes women get to give their testimony about the
miracle baby they were able to conceive against all odds.
Sometimes women end up like me and never have that
chance. I don't know why some women are able to have
children and some are not. I don't know why some women
are able to give their testimony and have their husbands
carry their miracle baby on the platform to show everyone,
while others like Sean and I would have to bring our child

onto the platform with a leash. I still have unanswered questions that I may never know the answers to.

What I do know is that I could have wallowed in my embarrassment and sadness, which would have been very easy to do. Or I could have sunk into depression because of feelings of embarrassment and failure. But I didn't. Here is what Sean and I decided to do instead:

- ✓ We began to look at travel magazines and watch travel shows that were exclusively for couples.
- ✓ We began having date nights and didn't need to first get a baby sitter.
- ✓ I took up photography again.
- ✓ We got not one, but two dogs—which we now refer to as our four-legged, hairy children when people ask us how many children we have.
- ✓ We go out to eat more . . . in fact, anytime we feel like it!
- ✓ I found that I really was happy to not have my period anymore.
- ✓ I minister to women and I love it!.
- ✓ I discovered that it is very rewarding for me to help people understand their loved one who is experiencing infertility.
- ✓ We spoil our niece and nephew as much as possible.

Don't get me wrong: I still have some healing to do. There are still times when I get tired of being asked how many children we have, because everyone is expected to have children. I still sometimes want to smack women who find out that we don't have any of our own children and laughingly offer us one of theirs. I find myself still turning off shows that have to do with pregnancy or giving birth.

But I am getting stronger every day. I find my strength through God, my husband, my family, and my friends. They say that time heals all wounds . . . it's just that some wounds take longer to heal than others.

Realizing that I had to deal with the loss as one dealing with a death in the family also has helped. I may not have ever actually given birth physically to our three children, but I did spiritually and emotionally, and I had to deal with the loss.

So whether you are reading this because of your daughter's struggle or your friend's struggle, remember to think before you speak and do a lot of listening.

If you are reading this book because it is you who is struggling, remember that *no one* knows just how you feel except you and God. So be forgiving, understand those who do not understand, and find things that make you happy that are not related to fertility or children.

Or, if your fertility journey ended as ours did, remember that we are all here for a reason . . . we all make a difference . . . and we can all live life after loss.

Althouth there are scriptures throughout the entire Bible that speak to us and what we are going through in life, the following verses have helped me to live life after loss, and I daily hold them in my heart.

Psalm 91:14-16

"Because he loves me." Says the Lord, "I will rescue him; I will protect him, for he acknowledges my name. He will call me, and I will answer him; I will be with him in trouble, I will deliver him and honor him. With long life will I satisfy him and show him my salvation."

Psalm 118:13-14

"I was pushed back and about to fall, but the Lord helped me. The Lord is my strength and my song; he has become my salvation."

Proverbs 3:4-5

"Trust in the lord with all your hear and lean not on your own understanding; in all your ways acknowledge him, and he will make your paths straight."

Jeremiah 29:11

"For I know the plans I have for you," declares the Lord, "plans to prosper you and not to harm you, plans to give you hope and a future."

Romans 8:28

"And we know that in all things God works for the good of those who love him, who have been called according to his purpose."

1 Corinthians 2:9

"However, as it is written: 'No eye has seen, no ear has heard, no mind has conceived what God has prepared for those who love him.'"

Philippians 3:13-14

"Brothers, I do not consider myself yet to have taken hold of it. But one thing I do: Forgetting what is behind and straining toward what is ahead, I press on toward the goal to win the prize for which God has called me heavenward in Christ Jesus."

Philippians 4:19

"And my God will meet all your needs according to his glorious riches in Christ Jesus."

1 Thessalonians 5:16–18

"Be joyful always, pray continually; give thanks in all circumstances, for this is God's will for you in Christ Jesus."

In Conclusion

As I stated in the introduction this book is not meant to treat or diagnose anyone currently experiencing difficulty conceiving. It is intended to help people better understand and support someone currently struggling through an infertility diagnosis or treatment.

For those of you who have a loved one experiencing trouble conceiving a child:

Remember that it can be a very frustrating and emotional journey. Your patience and love are invaluable in helping her through this uncertain time. You can't fix it for her, (no matter how much you want to) so don't try. What will mean more than anything is to just 'be there' for her. Give her a shoulder to cry on when she needs one. Just listen when she wants to talk or vent about what she is going through. Pray for her and her husband. And, finally . . . always ask her, "What can I do for you?".

For those of you who are experiencing the fertility rollercoaster yourselves:

Remember to take one day at a time. If I had one piece of advice for you, it would be to read Matthew 6:25-34 every day. The focus of theses verses is 'Do Not Worry'. Thinking back through all the years I spent worrying about everything day after day, I now ask myself, Why?". If I had only taken *one moment at a time* instead of always thinking about tomorrow, or the next day. If I had not spent so much time focusing on asking the "What if" and "Will I start my period this month . . . again?" questions. It is so easy to drown yourself in your quest to have a child, I know I did. I believe I missed living a lot of my life while focusing on what I believed to be the only life I wanted to live. Be careful to not put up any walls that prevent you from enjoying other people, and yes, other people's children. I'm not saying you should stop trying or give up. I did everything possible and have no regrets about how long we tried to have a child. I just wish I had continued to live my life *while* trying to have a child.

In closing, I wish you all the best. I hope that in some small way that this book has helped. If you would like to share your journey with me, I would love to hear from you. May God richly bless you.

Contact Information

To schedule Lisa for:

Health Seminars, Women's Ministry meetings,
Woman's Conferences or Church Services . . .

Visit Lisa on her Website:

Lisamurrayministries.org

Or Contact Her at:

lisa@lisamurrayministries.org